Ant Cestor™

Celebrates Kwanzaa

Story By Dan Moore, Sr.

Illustrated By
Jordan Solomon

ISBN-13:978-1503155190
ISBN-10:1503155196

Dedicated to all the children of the world. May we ever love and protect them.

Kwanzaa (KWAN-za) comes from the Swahili word Kwanza, which means first fruits.

Nguzo Saba (n-GU-zo SAH-bah) refers to the seven principles upon which Kwanzaa is based.

Hi, my name is Cedrick. I would like you to meet my father's sister. She is my aunt, Ant Cestor.

I just went to get the mail.
I was very careful going to
the mail box.

Ant Cestor told me the mail box was invented by a Black man in 1867. His name was Philip Downing. After all those years and we are still using it today.

From: Uncle Time
123 History Rd.
Ghana, West Africa

To: Cedrick
123 Ant Hill Place
USA

Wow. I have mail. It is from my Uncle Time. It came all the way from Ghana, West Africa.

And look, it has a very pretty stamp. It's a Kwanzaa stamp from America.

I can't wait to show it to my Ant Cestor.

Well," said Ant Cestor, you know
I love telling you about where we
all came from. Yes, we came from
Africa."

"There was a young man name Dr. Maulana Karenga. He lived in California.

"He loved to talk about his homeland, Africa. He studied a lot about his ancestors. We call them kin folks don't you know?"

"He knew it was important that we remember our roots. That means where we came from."

He studied about different African Societies. That is groups of people, from many villages."

"He took a little bit from each culture or group. Put them in a pot. Stirred them up and created the very first Kwanzaa.

"Now Kwanzaa is not to replace
Christmas. It is a celebration all its own.
It is taken from many African cultures,
or the way they do things.

"Dr. Karenga created a seven day celebration that would begin the day after Christmas and end on New Year's Day."

Each day we celebrate something different.

Umoja (oo-MO-jah)

The first day of Kwanzaa he called Umoja. That means Unity.

The second day of Kwanzaa is called Kujichagulia which means Self Determination. You decide to do something and then do it.

Ujamaa (oo-jah-MAH-ah

"The fourth day is Ujamaa and we learn to practice buying from people in our neighborhood.

Nia (NEE-ah)

"Day five is Nia. That means purpose. We must have a reason for the things we do. It is always good to do the right thing.

"Some words are hard to pronounce, but I remember everything you taught me," said Cedric.

"Yes," said Ant Cestor, "You are such a smart young lad." "Lad?" Cedric giggled." Ant Cestor, that's an old fashion word.

Ant Cestor just smiled. "Well, you will always be a lad to me. And a very good one I may add."

Imani (ee-MAH-nee}

"I remember the last day", shouted Cedric. "It's Imani. It means faith. And that's when we believe in a higher power, like our ancestors did.

"And I remember," said Cedric, "You told me that family comes together on this holiday celebration."

"They often give each other gifts. It's even better if the gifts are hand- made," said Ant Cestor.

"Kwanzaa is such a great celebration. I love to remember things from my ancestors", Ant Cestor, said to Cedric with a big smile.

This is how we celebrate Kwanzaa.

One of the first things we need is a candle holder. It's called a Kinara.

Next we need candles.
Remember never light candles
without the help of an adult.

We can set up a display. It will have a Kente cloth. It is pattern that comes from West Africa.

We can
add a
unity cup.

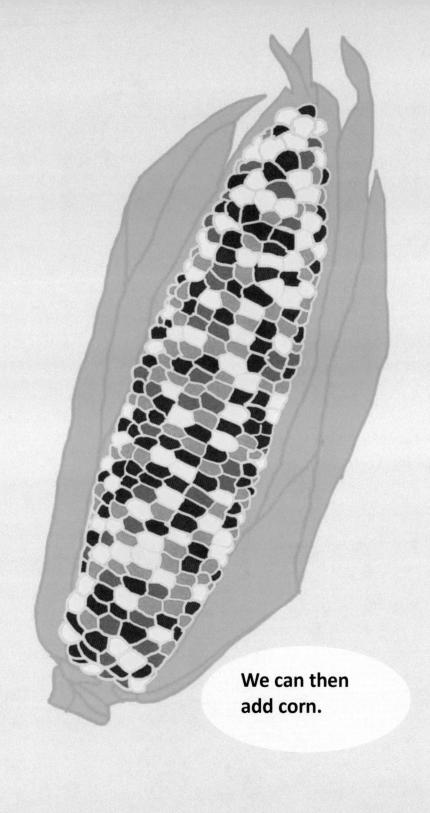

We can then add corn.

We can place all of these on a mat.

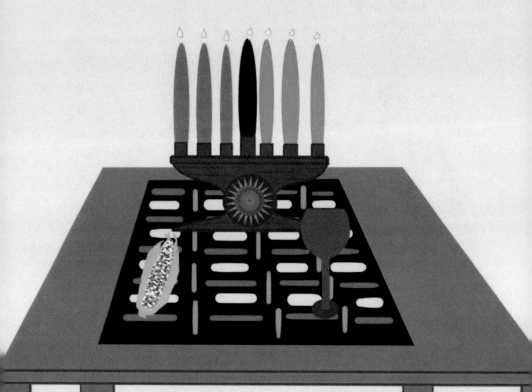

We now have a set up so we can
celebrate Kwanzaa.

Happy

Kwanzaa

Dr. Maulana Karenga

Dr. Maulana Karenga is professor and chair of Africana Studies at California State University, Long Beach. He is the creator of *Kwanzaa*, an African American and Pan-African holiday celebrated throughout the world African community on every continent in the world. *Kwanzaa is a Celebration of Family, Community and Culture.*

For more information on Dr. Karenga and Kwanza visit his website
http://www.officialkwanzaawebsite.org

Dr. Synthia SAINT JAMES

Synthia SAINT JAMES is a world renowned multicultural visual artist, award winning author and or illustrator of 17 children's books, authored an autobiographical art marketing book, 3 poetry books, a book of affirmations, and a cookbook.

She is most celebrated for designing the first Kwanzaa Stamp for the United States Postal Service in 1997.

www.synthiasaintjames.com

Made in the USA
Columbia, SC
27 October 2021